thirsty

thirsty

DIONNE BRAND

McCLELLAND & STEWART

Library and Archives Canada Cataloguing in Publication

Brand, Dionne, 1953-
Thirsty

Poems.
ISBN 978-0-7710-1644-8

I. Title.

PS8553.R275T55 2002   C811'.54   C2002-900282-6
PR9199.3.R275T55 2002

We acknowledge the financial support of the Government of Canada through the Book Publishing Industry Development Program for our publishing activities. We further acknowledge the support of the Canada Council for the Arts and the Ontario Arts Council for our publishing program.

Typeset in Bembo by M&S, Toronto
Printed and bound in the USA

McClelland & Stewart,
a division of Penguin Random House Canada Limited,
a Penguin Random House Company
www.penguinrandomhouse.ca

5 6 7 8 9   18 17 16

To Leleti

I

This city is beauty
unbreakable and amorous as eyelids,
in the streets, pressed with fierce departures,
submerged landings,
I am innocent as thresholds
and smashed night birds, lovesick,
as empty elevators

let me declare doorways,
corners, pursuit, let me say
standing here in eyelashes, in
invisible breasts, in the shrinking lake
in the tiny shops of untrue recollections,
the brittle, gnawed life we live,
I am held, and held

the touch of everything blushes me,
pigeons and wrecked boys,
half-dead hours, blind musicians,
inconclusive women in bruised dresses
even the habitual grey-suited men with terrible
briefcases, how come, how come
I anticipate nothing as intimate as history

would I have had a different life
failing this embrace with broken things,
iridescent veins, ecstatic bullets, small cracks
in the brain, would I know these particular facts,
how a phrase scars a cheek, how water
dries love out, this, a thought as casual
as any second eviscerates a breath

and this, we meet in careless intervals,
in coffee bars, gas stations, in prosthetic
conversations, lotteries, untranslatable
mouths, in versions of what we may be,
a tremor of the hand in the realization
of endings, a glancing blow of tears
on skin, the keen dismissal in speed

II

There was a Sunday morning scent,
an early morning air, then the unarranged light
that hovers on a street before a city wakes
unrelieved to the war fumes of fuel exhaust

The city was empty, except for the three,
they seemed therefore poised, as when you are alone
anywhere all movement is arrested, light, dun,
except, their hearts, scintillant as darkness

clothy blooms of magnolia, bedraggled shrubs,
wept over a past winter, a car sped by,
scatterling from sleep, their mirage disquiets,
the subway, tumescent, expectant like a grave

They had hoped without salvation for a trolley,
they arrived at the corner impious, then,
wracked on the psalmody of the crossroad,
they felt, the absences of a morning

They circled sovereign thoughts, taking
for granted the morning, the solidity of things,
the bank to one corner, the driving school on another,
the milk store and the church

each her own separate weight,
each carried it in some drenched region of flesh,
the calculus of silence, its chaos,
the wraith and rate of absence pierced them

Chloe bathed in black, then the youngest,
leather bag strapped to a still school
girlish back, the last a precise look to her yet,
a violet lace, a hackle from forehead to neck

captured in individual doubt, a hesitation,
and what they could not put into words,
indevotion, on this eighteenth Sunday
every cool black-dressed year since 1980

This slender lacuna beguiles them,
a man frothing a biblical lexis at Christie
Pits, the small barren incline where his mad sermons
cursed bewildered subway riders, his faith unstrained

then nothing of him but his parched body's declension
a curved caesura, mangled with clippers, and
clematis cirrhosa and a budding grape vine he was still
to plant when he could, saying when he had fallen, ". . . thirsty . . ."

III

That north burnt country ran me down
to the city, mordant as it is, the whole
terror of nights with yourself and what
will happen, animus, loose like that, sweeps
you to embrace its urban meter,
the caustic piss of streets,
you surrender your heart to a numb symmetry
of procedures, you study the metaphysics of
corporate instructions and not just,
besieged by now, the ragged, serrated theories
of dreams walking by, banked in sleep

that wild waiting at traffic lights off
the end of the world, where nothing is simple,
nothing, in the city there is no simple love
or simple fidelity, the heart is slippery,
the body convulsive with disguises
abandonments, everything is emptied,
wrappers, coffee cups, discarded shoes,
trucks, street corners, shop windows, cigarette
ends, lungs, ribs, eyes, love,
the exquisite rush of nothing,
the damaged horizon of skyscraping walls,
nights insomniac with pinholes of light

IV

History doesn't enter here, life, if you call it that,
on this small street is inconsequential,
Julia, worked at testing cultures and the stingy
task, in every way irredeemable, of saving money

Then Alan came, his mother, left, came ill
squeezing a sewing machine into a hallway
and then the baby. Already you can see how
joylessness took a hold pretending to be joy

Once she had risen, reprieved from the humus subway,
heard his sermonizing, sent to her by the wind
on the harp of children and leaves and engines,
she bolted the sound of his voice pursuing

She had been expecting happiness with him, why not
a ravishing measureless happiness, he spilled instead
suspicions on her belly, where was the money
she was saving, where the light she was keeping from his hands

She would waken to find the luminous filament
of his cigarette, he rage red as the tip,
weeping, he couldn't take it any more. Then threats.
She tried tenderness. What? She must take him for a fool

The worn velvet, the late condolences
for a thing buried long before his death. Julia
sees malediction in the sly crucifix,
her back bent over specimens plotting rapture

V

That polychromatic murmur, the dizzying
waves, the noise of it, the noise of it
was the first thing. There was too
an unremitting light, through the window,
through the darkness, there was no darkness,
a steady drizzle of brightness, falling
but sleep, suddenly in the middle of it,
sleep. I woke up these mornings thinking, how
could it be rest, this clamour, but rest,
the neighbour with the vacuum cleaner and the baby
and the television's basilisk stare,
the sportscaster so sleepless,
his medicine, more noise, the fridge groaning
from the weight of ice, and the dog
wounded with absence howling downstairs

the silvery rasp of my lungs begins
to resemble everything, more engines
and stranded birds, decayed chocolate,
windscreens, my blood, a jackhammer
of breaking stars, the light again, tenacious

VI

The neighbours complained that he borrowed, took things,
rakes, saws, gloves, shovels, flowers, weeds – without asking
one tulip, three peonies, seven irises,
the devil, he said, was all in the world, abroad, he said,
his face in the quivering of baby's breath,
hold my hand, he told his daughter, the devil can't come between us

The sewing machine starting up when he left, chasing zippers,
his mother blamed her. Some proper thing Julia hadn't done,
an incantation for his un-magic life,
her good, good son had been spoiled
and there had to be blame for his distress,
hers too, threaded and buttoned between her teeth

The cornflowers, the yarrow, the lavender, the wild chamomile,
his living face in her purse. A smiling man in a double
breasted suit, his hair flared to the finger-worn corners
of the picture. He'd sent this likeness long ago to say
that he was doing well

VII

That flutter in her hand started then.
Out the door into the damp May light,
Julia looks south to the magnolia bushes,
she feels their petals in her mouth
she reaches, puts them on her tongue

she is standing on the church steps
tasting the fiction of magnolia blossoms,
another year, she had reckoned silence
might dull the meaning, it would subside
like a sentence should. But it hadn't.

She pretends fixing an imaginary seam
settling a toque on her wintry head,
she's spent her time finding things
for her runaway hand to do. All seasons.

She has become used to its rhythms,
except in public it escapes,
had she willed him to vanish? had she
a passion so hidden it happened, as passions do

tethered to this city block, this church,
these spring blossoms on her tongue,
what if she disappears into another city,
she could taste again the ordinariness of coffee
take as small but sufficient a ride on a bus

toward a named street, she could head into
her life with the same ferocity as anyone,
wake up to the pillowed hush of a snowy morning,
burrow the greyness of seven o'clock in December,
if she had not been so hasty as to get Alan killed

VIII

now the door faces nothing, the window faces nothing
a parking lot, a toxic shed where movies
are made, a bus stop where pigeons light
between the morning crowd and the afternoon
itinerant baby and girl-mother,
they've laid a quick over green sod down
back of this urban barracoon, hoping
to affect beauty, no books this time, no
dictionaries to hang on to, just me and the city
that's never happened before, and happened
though not ever like this, the garbage
of pizza boxes, dead couches,
the strip mall of ambitious immigrants
under carcasses of cars, oil-soaked
clothing, hulks of rusted trucks, scraggily
gardens of beans, inshallahs under the breath,
querido, blood fire, striving stilettoed rudbeckia

breathing, you can breathe if you find air,
this roiling, this weight of bodies,
as if we need each other to breathe, to bring
it into sense, and well, in that we are merciless

IX

i

It would matter to know him as a child,
after all, he's dead when this begins
and no one so far has said a word about him
that wasn't somehow immaculate with his disaster

He was swept into a passion by the smallest injury,
would weep at a trail of ants spurning his friendship,
a boy as any who would mope if his teacher did not pick him
to clean the blackboard, ferreting bits of chalk

Everything he did was half done out of eagerness,
his homework, his half-buttoned shirt his half-shod feet,
everything he did he did hurriedly anticipating
what never measured his need

At sixteen the astonished foreman sucked his teeth
forgave the boy putting too much water in the concrete
and writing his name over and over again in the drying
pavement. Two weeks of money in mistakes and surliness

got him sent home to his mother. It wasn't complicated
she told him, it was as simple as a straight stitch,
showing him the chastened yellow cloth under her presser-foot,
"The world don't value good people," she told him

"The world don't value good people." A definite path,
he had seized first on a girl, like an anchor,
full knowing that he could not summon love
or surety in anyone. He could not flower passion

just as he knew he could not spring wild mimosa in Toronto,
the bible to steady him then, never a person for edges

and uncertainties, he only wanted a calming loving spot,
we all want that but the world doesn't love you

ii

All the dreadfulness that happened in America had happened,
his inspired sermons at Christie Pits steamed,
a baby found in a microwave, a baby shaken to death,
fourteen girls murdered in a college, people kidnapped,

Black men dragged, two, three young girls tortured
and raped and killed by a sweet blond boy,
bodies found in lakes and forests, bodies in car trunks,
bodies god knows where in disappearances,

the child killers in high schools, the rages on the highways,
the pushing murders in subways, killers in the street,
the brain-numbing dress rehearsals for victims and predators on TV,
well then, all this dreadfulness had come home to him

X

i

If withdrawal is an emotion, well then,
the vault of her hands pried open
to form the gesture of love required, if not
given whole, she glistens like disappearance

through the city, its own weight made up
of vanishings, she reaches her bicycle locked
near the church, she glides only to its clicking
wheels, not to the clatter of their various sorrow

on the stone steps, in dresses formidably black,
and a ruff of pale violet, a crisp hat, a thin lace
veil, a hand rustling and rustling, the sacrificial
breaths, hasping the shutter of lungs

this morning, in a house long abandoned
she saw the doorway sheeted in the lint
of spiders, the dusty light, the crumbling braces,
the man falling down saying, "thirsty"

ii

She thinks of turning around perhaps waving,
as if this was not a departure,
as if it were a temporary and recoverable distance
she wants to turn around with a duty done

and therefore a happiness, well,
the gears are already silvery
with abandonment, cutting out the route to
leaving them, a geomancy of the smallest damages.

iii

This time of year was treacherous as sermons
if arriving ready for a cleaning lament,
the threnody of her winter-stored bicycle tuned,
for a man who died and was cherished with flowers,

chrysanthemums, white, her mother fluttered,
had they shared some conspiracy?
this, commingled with her gaze eternally
childish. The wake, the remembrance eclipsed

iv

"What did you do?" this shivered
unsaid, she had found herself
grasped for and held and, "Did I?"
was it when she stood at the window

in the small celebrity of her father's falling,
then she would have to forgive herself childhood
and childhood had become circumstantial,
all part, the reason that he fell.

All this passes between them this morning,
but this morning in her mother's flailing,
it had inexplicably shone beneath the usual
lace veil. There had been defiance there before,

steeliness, exasperation, impassivity. Not
long-suffering. She is pure energy,
she can light the gloomy church and illuminate
the dead street just opening her mouth

and if she lingers they will burn up in her breath,
she is a wave of hot light, she needs a bicycle,
a sparrow of light, and meter, velocity itself,
she hurtles out of this lamentation to her only life

XI

i

you can't satisfy people, we long for everything,
but sleep, sleep is the gift of the city
the breath of others, their mewling, their disorder,
I could hear languages in the lush smog,
runes to mercy and failure and something tender
a fragile light, no, not light, yes light,
something you can put your hand in, relinquishing

I'll tell you this. I've seen a toxic sunset,
flying down over the city, its gorgeous spit
licking the airplane, how it is that steel weeps
with the sense of bodies, pressed, another passion,
we become other humans,
boisterous and metallic, fibrous and deserted.
Here I could know nothing and live,
harbour a dead heart,
slip corrosive hands into a coat

ii

These are the muscles of the subway's syrinx
Vilnus, Dagupan, Shaowu, Valparaiso, Falmouth, and Asmara.
The tunnel breathes in the coming train exhaling
as minerals the grammar of Calcutta, Colombo,
Jakarta, Mogila and Senhor do Bonfim, Ribeira Grande
and Hong Kong, Mogadishu and the alias St. Petersburg

the city keens its rough sonancy,
you would be mistaken to take it as music
it is the sound before music
when the throat vomits prehistoric birds

XII

It was late spring then, it was warm already,
he, jeremiad at the door holding the rough bible
to his temple like rhymed stone, she the last bolt
in her head shut, "Alan, let me pass."
"Oh my god!" his mother foretelling the meter,
he versed, "You're not leaving here with what is mine,"

her heart travelled the short distance of their joy
all the anger she had vaulted like gold belongings,
"Call the police! child, call the police! 911!"
The rake? The gloves? Had they come for the neighbours' things?
the tulip, the infinitesimal petals of spirea, the blossoms
he kissed this morning? "Here, wait." Then he would give them
their clippers, the branches of lilacs, the watering hose,
the two lengths of wild grasses that came off his hands.

They couldn't have come here to his house to stop him
from quarrelling with his own wife, it was the clippers
or the rake or their garden hose. He would straighten
things out, he would confess to the poppies, the white astilbe
Julia was leaving and no way she was taking what was his,
declaring the hedge clippers he said, "Look take it . . ."

"What the devil . . ." already descending.
"What the devil you all making so much noise for?"
then his chest flowered stigma of scarlet bergamot
their petal tips prickled his shirt, spread to his darkening
throat, he dropped the clippers to hold his breaking face,
he felt dry, "Jesus . . . thirsty . . ." he called, falling.

XIII

I don't remember that frail morning, how
could I? No one wakes up thinking of a stranger,
a life away, falling. I don't recall the
morning at all, as urgent or remarkable, though
falling was somehow predictable, but only when
you think of it later, falling is all you can do,
as hereditary as thirst, and so of course
he was thirsty, as I, craving a slake of baby's
breath, or bergamot, though we were not the same,
god would not be sufficient for me,
nor the ache and panic of a city surprising,
but thirst I know, and falling, thirst for fragrant
books, a waiting peace, for life, for just halting,
so I could breathe an air less rancid, live, anonymously

so no I don't recall the day, why would I? Let
alone, I've been busy with my own life, you have
to be on your toes or else you'll drown
in the thought of your own diminishing, as I said
I crave of course being human as he must have
and she, but not to let it get away with you,
don't dwell too long, don't stand still here,
I skim, I desert, I break off the edges,
I believe nothing, I dream but that's free

XIV

Her hand leafs through the grained air
of the room gleaning strands of his breath
and something to be put back together
and his mother's tuning wail and the dark

blue of the policemen's uniforms,
it touches shoes and the stairway
and a going bliss, the polish
of a dimming effort and a hint of
scarlet bergamot, in . . . here take them

Alan is in cinders on the floor,
she herself is smoldering with her
own incandescence, her reach for what
she must keep and the child to steady her

XV

All the hope gone hard. That is a city.
The blind houses, the cramped dirt, the broken
air, the sweet ugliness, the blissful and tortured
flowers, the misguided clothing, the bricked lies
the steel lies, all the lies seeping from flesh
falling in rain and snow, the weeping buses,
the plastic throats, the perfumed garbage, the
needled sky, the smogged oxygen, the deathly clerical
gentlemen cleaning their fingernails at the stock
exchange, the dingy hearts in the newsrooms, that is
a city, the feral amnesia of us all

Other people standing on this step at the church door
would wedge loss in their mouths like a soother,
but they had not had a big life and therefore a life
that could be interrupted by Alan falling,

a life that would recover, they had not had a life
that could rebound. Some had lives like that,
an expected death or, perhaps, a devastating accident,
this was beyond any small drama of tears

Newsprint would record her dry eyes,
would catch, in the middle of a flutter,
her index finger curling, the rest,
cascading neo-impressionist rage,

as if an urgent Seurat had appeared at the funeral
his pointillist blaze touching the minute light
of her heart for his *Models*, this death,
the vacant occasion of a painting

Readers would seek grief there, they would
not be prepared for emptiness such as hers,
At the moment when her nude portrait was complete
small things like the dusty cupboard to be washed

or the child's coat thinning or a certain car
revving its engine annoyingly crossed her face,
and so readers may have seen indifference
and when the back of her black funeral shoes

severed her skin they may have generously mistaken it
for a twinge of pain, when she remembered a good hot cup
of coffee she had had at five o'clock in the morning
like any spectator they may have seen satisfaction

and then again when she was tired of Alan's mother crying
they may have read exasperation with it all,
they would not be used to the concept of emptiness
selvedged with the science of darkness and light

as from any woman put together by newsprint,
mourners expected tears, and so she would have
appeared a hard woman, save she would know
the genuine sign of her own laser keen self-disgust

XVII

It isn't, it really isn't
the city, brief as history,
but my life in it passing sooner
than this thirst is finished, I
can offer nothing except a few glances
an uneasy sleep, a wild keening,
it would appear nothing said matters,
nothing lived, but, this is my occupation.
One day I will record the tenses of light,
not now

XVIII

Around them the city is waking up as a girl vanishes
as light,
two women feel limbless, handless, motionless
what will they do now

It is only she that brings them to any life,
makes them
understand what day it is and that perhaps
things may pass

since that day which they are still standing in,
skinless.
Time starts with her and ends when she leaves
and even

if she vanishes on her bicycle of light,
when all
she is occupied with is fleeing them, they know
much more is gone

She will return to set them in motion, they hope
they will tell her,
they will confess their loneliness, they will
promise her

all the promises on their lips, to forget, to patch it
up, to carry on.
They will dream for her all the things people dream
for people they love

they will dream her first kiss, they will dream her
graduation from college,
they will dream her wedding, they will dream her children,
if only

she would turn around and look for them. Their eyes
are eager,
their hands waiting to smooth her wedding dress, to button
her satin shoes,

to pat her hair. They lust to kiss her husband,
to tell him
he must be careful with their girl, she's the only daughter
they have

they will love
his dark face, his even skin, his staggering smile.
She will turn
around they wish, each elated, each ready

they think
to make it right if only she does, to start anew.
They imagine each
that they will be ready with a rare laugh if she turns

and if she comes back
each plans to forgive the other, not to quibble
as to whom
she loves more or whom she smiles at first. They are breathless

for her
and they think that the picture of them standing there
must seem exultant
and deserving of her and without despair. They could both

attest
in that moment to representing branches and fire and flight.
Fleeing.
Is fleeing what the curve of her back means? Is there shrinking

The street begins
to move, and they are caught in an abrupt wind, the traffic
summing up
itself to its usual rush, the life around them pearls

against their grain
until they are stems on which dresses gust and fly, leaves
caught
in another time, in the middle of life they are an outskirt.

They've gathered all their fragile veins
and if only
she were to come back she would see them in full blood.
But to anyone walking

by, they are unslaked as ghosts.
They cannot summon hope though they are bursting with it,
it is so subterranean
it cannot break the surface of their skin, it cannot lap

their waiting arms
and overwhelm their failures, as it must
were she
to look back to their exact vision,

one solidly inconsolable, the other all dead flutter.
The street
now in full flight, no one notices that they are arrested,
waiting for a return

People bump against them, a murmured "sorry" cannot know
how appropriate it is,
an impatient brushing, cannot truly feel
their immobility

XIX

i

They had been observed by a man with unusual kindness
for a city. He had sensed the extravagant calm
where an old woman leaned on a cane. He had seen

the rest of the street as if blowing by in a windstorm,
he, swept up in it on his way to the halal store,
thinks of his own mother on the road in Jaffna

confused amid the mad morning traffic, her smallness
in peril on the corner of Hospital Vithi,
he has not seen her since one bird-silent day when

he left home, fleeing, himself. He keeps a register
of her face, transparent as terror in his walking
dreams on Bloor Street

He reaches to embrace Chloe, the sameness of his love
falls on her, his hands anticipate the doves of her
arms, the warming sobs she wipes from his face

but then he notices a black-winged stillness, a
violet lace-covered eyes with the merest tremor
so he passes

ii

They had been observed too by a woman
if only because she was as jittery as they were quiet,
she had awakened to a hard burning in her veins

she had grabbed her homeless skin, too thick
for the warm spring, too flimsy for her shiver,
she was trying to cop an early dime

she would not have noticed them but only noticed
as the fastest thing notices the slowest,
as they are in synergy with each other

she was sweating, they ice cool,
as stars bursting slowly in the speeding universe,
she in a quick burn, they singed

her hair falls lank, her sweat corrodes her cheeks,
she scratches the furious pox of crack raw,
cancres open to the god of the terrible morning

Sault Ste. Marie is where her vowels abandoned her,
a car ride hopped on acid and well needed gasoline
left her at half the journey to this city block

speechless, only the wrought skeleton that now was
her face, jabbed the air. She would love to stop
her own breath and the story it drowns in

they, heavy black and invisible violet cruised
her eyebrow along with the thought of her hookup,
she wanted to be that languid,

spots her jones man in the blue phone booth
half a block down and flies, bowed out of their orbit
a wrecked moon. She hopes this hit will last eternity

iii

Their cocoon becomes porous letting in the murmuring city,
the cars gunning at the traffic light, the war of daylight,
waiting, painless, if only that girl would turn around and come home

XX

Consider the din of beginnings, this vagrant, fugitive city
just hours ago these people standing prone as sleep
in subways were enclosed in the silk of their origins,
glowing chrysalises of old, at least, inconvenient cultures

they had some set notions of who they were, buried in apartments
and houses in North York and Scarborough and Pickering,
those suburbs undifferentiated, prefabricated from no great
narrative, except cash, there is no truth to their names

they don't even vaguely resemble the small damp villages
of their etymology. The Romans would not build roads here,
unflagging dreariness dries the landscape, meagre oases of woodland
fight gas stations and donut shops for any thing named beauty

Thomson would have snatched his *Burnt Country* away from here,
knowing that it would vanish. This suburban parching would dry bog
far more succour the oversleeping, the insomniac, summer wastes,
mauve light, mauve, mauve dark black, mauve white, reconstructing

what they choose to remember and what they mis-forget of places
they'd known. They are improvising as Lismer's *Forest in Winter*
some recent past, drowned hues, drenched schemes, plans,
for an arranged marriage, a red bride, a white garlanded groom, the

Gurdwara on Weston Road. Blue, blue, blue black, that brilliant
red leafed tree, yellow leafed tree, the immigrant from Sheffield,
Lismer paints Sackville River with the same new memory as Violet
Blackman, her gesso was that wood floor in Rosedale

1920, when Toronto was just a village and all her labour, all her
time, all her heart and hand could not make that painting work, so,
hanging on fading histories, igniting another burnt drama
forty years from St. Elizabeth someone says this is how we do

christenings back home yet longs to see the world over, elsewhere
someone disciplined a son coming home, too late, "We live here
but don't think that we're going to live like people here!"
The city's cathedral of smogged sky receives the daily sacrament

of conditional sentences about conditional places, "If we were home.
I would . . ." as strong a romance with the past tense as with what is
to come. Cresting as the engraver's mountain red black, purple, light
suffused in sunset, important in the middle of the pluperfect

in the subway though these separate dreamers are a mass of silences.
They are echo chambers for the voices of the gods of
cities. Glass, money, goods. They sit in a universe of halted breaths
waiting for this stop Bay and that stop Yonge and that one St. Patrick

in early morning surrender to factories in Brampton,
swirling grey into the 401 and the Queen Elizabeth Highway,
they hold their tempers, their passions, over grumbling machines
until night, dreaming their small empires, their domestic tyrannies

but of course no voyage is seamless. Nothing in a city is discrete.
A city is all interpolation. The Filipina nurse bathes a body, the
Vincentian courier delivers a message, the Sikh cab driver navigates a
corner. What happens? A new road is cut, a sound escapes, a touch
lasts

XXI

i

The house is still there, on Hallam Street,
still half-sleeping, ramshackled like wintering
bear. Days after her father fell and his mother
folded beside him, there had been the funeral

"Poor child, poor child, . . . to have to see that . . ."
Chloe, sopping her head with bay leaves and rum,
discovered her sanguine, and put an end to it,
"Cry! I tell you, you unmerciful child."

A slow black car took them to his funeral,
a crowd impassioned in black and white
and beige and purple followed. Heavy, palms,
poured a veil of fingers over her eyes

Chloe sang *By the Rivers of Babylon,*
then broke like cake into tears,
cracked into a falsetto of grief
raised in the air to summon an inattentive God

the procession not anything like mourning, but
a fury took her father's incline at Christie Pits,
a loudspeaker quavered, ". . . did not deserve
in his own house   no peace   before

his child   the Toronto police
have to answer   any one of us
time and again
not going to stand   justice for our brother,"
the wife's face was waterless though

ii

Each May after for eighteen Mays she came to the moment
her husband fiercely beatific in the beige tucked coffin
as if he had expected the inconsolable casket,
and their life after, draped dim with his radiance
yet that moment, that moment she felt nothing at all

and nothing since. Leading to this May and previous
with the three of them left. They were alone in the world.
Which really was how they'd felt in the first place
before Alan fell down whispering, ". . . thirsty . . ."

which is to say, human. I did hear the city's susurrus,
loud, wide, promising, like wine, obscurity and rapture,
the bright veiled Somali women hyphenating Scarlett Road,
the eternal widows, Azorean and Italian at Igreja de Santa
Inez and Iglesia de San Antonio. At the Sea King Fish Market,
the Portuguese men have learned another language. "Yes
sweetie, yes dahling, and for you only this good good price."
This to the old Jamaican women who ask, "Did you cut the fish
like I told you? Why you charging me so much?" This dancing,
these presences, not the least, writing the biographies
of streets, I took, why not, yes, as wonderful

summer teems, College and Bathurst, Queen and Yonge,
St. Clair and Dufferin, Eglinton to the highway,
at these crossroads, transient selves flare
in the individual drama, in the faith of translation,
at the covert dance halls, at the cut-rate overpriced
shopping malls, there are impossible citizens,
repositories of the city's panic, there are those
here too worn as if by brutal winds, a pocked
whale-boned, autumnal arctic stone of a face,
not wind at all but some unproven element works
there, Spadina and Bloor to the Mission
and the Silver Dollar south, unproven, not unseen

XXIII

I'll tell you what I've seen here at Yonge and Bloor,
At this crossroad, the air is elegiac with it
whiffs and cirri of all emotion, need and vanity,
desire, brazen as a killing

a burger a leather jacket a pair of shoes a smoke
to find a job to get drunk at the Zanzibar,
a body the body of a woman in a cage on the window
in a photograph in a strip joint two blocks away.

to piss to get drunk to get fucked to get high
grease sushi men wanting to be beaten to be touched
and all the anonymous things that may happen
on a corner like this for instance murder

If you look into any face here you might fall
into its particular need. And a woman I've seen her
Julia perhaps walks here I can't quite make her out
She is a mixture of twigs and ink she's like paper

XXIV

In the kitchen her tongue parts the flesh of avocados
and ackees,
the stiff tough saltiness of dried cod; the waves of chatter
are light

her teeth crush the meat of milk coconuts, sever the hairs
of mangoes
Oh she cultivated this light talk,
nothing wrong,

as if Alan would break the door any minute coming home.
Inaudible, frothy
and insensible, the words never deep enough to get at the matter
just enough

this talk, enough to fill, enough to circle the knowing, not hurdle
the last thing they shared
in all this time no word of condolence, not cursing or strain
of last night's restless sleep

words
were the opposite of meaning in this house now,
the meter
of Julia's hand more intuitive than any set of sounds
gathering

too busy
to cook dinner, that hand dancing with her mouth, her neck
it keeps
reaching out for the phone, dialing and dialing, circumnavigating

that bolt
of white light speeding away on a bicycle, yesterday,
she had lost
her hold, she had allowed an emotion. She had merely felt affinity

for the magnolias
then she'd turned her face, adjusted her hair, an expression
of self-pity had moved her muscles.
That's all.

If she would suddenly walk to the corner of Yonge
and Bloor
supposing there the incessant movement of her hand
would subside

or melt in the solitary flights, the syllables of weeping
collected there
might slake her might swamp her might breathe
her heart wet

perhaps there, this suffocating sacrifice to everyone
this city
the falling man, the withering readers, the absent mourners
might stop

and there the smell of flowers less melancholy
Mays turned
furious with her living body, a scythed moon ravished
in neon

there as she always planned, the trembling
timbre of gathered
dreams, a small apartment with music and perhaps
a bird

if she could bear the cage, but there a sense
of flight in green
some songs. Only something small as a winter
a twilight

without that mistake, the look she had misjudged
so terribly
as reflecting her own fabulous, now,
purpose

happiness. Why did she need forgiveness for that
for air
for the temperature of her thoughts, the weather
of her flesh

passion,
she's seen it under a microscope in a laboratory
ferocious
spilling on her hand, a wave she should follow

a ride
on the ferry to Hanlan's Point, nakedness
she needed
could find some place to be naked, to slip her body

becoming
transparent as veins and letters and children
fugitive
as crossroads and windowpanes and bread

and blue
this sweet colour in skies and paintings
she
would simply exist for

XXV

After he was thirsty the sewing machine fell silent
for quite a while, at odd hours as if struck, some sudden
pain, a word wailed like "my . . ." so haunched

other times a raucous peeping like a small bird
weeping for hours and days, then one day the sewing
machine started up again and never seemed to stop still

the floor littered in threads and odds and ends of long
haired cloth. The child loved the taste of threads, the
treat of buttons, the disorderliness, recondite blooms

smothered in bottomless cloth treading her way, great
arms not enough to keep the cloth from suffocating her,
the machine not quick enough to keep up with her desire

"God did what God did." The man who had shot her son,
may he live in hell. She had accounted, read his name
into Psalm 37, "For they shall soon be cut down like the grass,"

Only that and verse one, "Fret not thyself because of evil
doers," had stopped her from delivering him home.
In the courthouse yard a happiness washing his face

she, Chloe had rushed at him with her bare hands.
There was no shame in some people. After all every
body is human, everybody wants forgiveness

she had been willing to forgive if he asked her,
she had felt it within her power to kill him
and to forgive him. She held back balancing this power

XXVI

So, a cop sashaying from a courthouse,
his moustache wide and bristling,
his wool coat draped across his body
and carefree, his head centred in the television
cameras against
scales of justice, he would strike
a match on the bottom of his shoes,
light a cigar in victory of being acquitted
of such a killing, and why not

captured by several television networks,
a vulgarity to it, a sybaritic languor
the guy walks toward his visual audience
as a high-fashion model walking a couture runway
in Paris or Milan. A showy stride
with the sexy swagger of a male model,
all muscle and grace, his virility in hand
his striking the match like a gunslinger,
this élan, law and outlaw, SWAT and midnight rider,
history and modernity kissing here

XXVII

i

The television tuned to the perpetual gospel channel
has worn out, its florid pigments washed cadaverous yellow,
she's fallen asleep to it and awakened to it every day

the preacher is reading from First Corinthians, chapter 13,
his Texan psaltery whining, "But when that which is perfect
is come, then that which is in part shall be done away."

God doesn't give you what you can't handle. Yesterday
stiff with hope she knew the clear thing as soon as the morning
disappeared, she could not reach into another generation

she didn't have to. Sprawled insensible on the mounds of cloth
Chloe murmurs this insight to the air above her face
The Texan evangelist confirms, "When that . . . is come . . ."

Chloe isn't waking up this morning. The tube will soon burn out
on the television, its blanched light and its voice,
Chloe never bothered with the converter once the battery was gone

the televangelists were all her interest anyway and the soap
operas. The sprockets on the tuning switch smoothed
the television had arrived at a vacant rest on the prayer channel

It doesn't matter. She's not waking up to try and catch
Days of Our Lives. The Texan minister is at verse twelve
of First Corinthians when Chloe crosses herself in her sleep

by this time today Chloe would have been awake, drunk a cup
of coffee, had a secret cigarette or two, and listened
to the apartment for evidence of her son.

He would have asked her to braid his hair, she would have
made rows around her fingers; she would have scratched his scalp,
he would have fallen asleep in her hands.

ii

She is elsewhere, by a river, the Rio Cobre, pitching stones,
she is dressed in her whole slip, Alan big in her belly,
she dives into the water becoming weightless,
that is when she crosses her arms in her sleep

and she is climbing a hilly road, thankful
that the day is rainy and cool; the grass and trees
and their colonies of insects and birds, all she hears,
her legs are bare and young she takes the road

now ahead of her in the distance, a small boy, a bag
on his shoulder, kicking pebbles and dust,
skitters down the stairs with the hedge clippers
and she is wiping the floor around his head in threads

the knitwear company is ringing the doorbell again
and Chloe hears the small coins she's given Alan
they are jingling in the pocket of his short blue pants.
That girl has written. She's sent his ticket. He'll be leaving soon

There's a siren sound in Chloe's sleep
and she thinks in her dream, "Whose life is that?"
The scar on her index finger from the sewing machine
is healed evangelically. Completely.

The television is seeing its own last doorway,
the evangelist now a woman with healing powers
she's sent that woman cash money for her good works,
addressed her divine ministry in Atlanta, Georgia

off this road Chloe isn't waking up,
this motionless morning, things will come
to rest, the thread dust, the cloth dust,
the May light is streaming into Chloe's room

XXVIII

Anyone, anyone can find themselves on a street corner
eclipsed, as they, by what deserted them
volumes of blue skirt with lace eyelets
a dance stroke you might have trimmed
the way a day can slip out of your hand,
your senses spill like water,
the tremolos of Leroy Jenkins' violin exiting
the Horseshoe Tavern, the accumulation of tender
seconds you should have noticed, as mercy,
even these confessions of failure so unreliable,
hardly matter

A house in this city is a witness box
of every kind of human foolishness
and then it all passes, new people inhabit
old occurrences are forgotten and
repeated to be forgotten again.
Before them a girl had died here of leukemia,
a thirteen year old, she liked jigsaw puzzles
she died hard, like Chloe's son,
well perhaps his was harder

No one prepares for how he died,
no one had a diagnosis beforehand
unless you count the mere presence of him,
his likeness, unless you count that
as a symptom of what he would die of,
unless you count a moment on a staircase
when guesses searing as letters
turned his face into a nightmare
instead of the face of Chloe's boy
who was afraid of his own shadow
and in a panic about losing everything

The girl who died here was born
in Regio Calabria,
though she spoke English when she was ill
and no one understood
she was a pretty girl and the leukemia
made her curiously prettier,
in sickness her beauty was so convincing
they could not open her casket for fear
she would come alive again through beauty

It isn't a haunting. That would be too fabulous.
It happened and what happened, happened.

Nothing unfortunately is ever one way,
juice, jam, yogurt, milk, everything spilled
on that spot before Alan's head did.
A deliberate red, like Ethiopian henna,
seeped into the floor grooves when Alan fell

The walls of a house can sense like skin,
that is why sometimes you can tell
what happened in this apartment,
the doorway shivers a deep blue, the ceilings rain,
the staircase declares a radiant girl
and someone saying, "thirsty . . ."

XXX

Spring darkness is forgiving. It doesn't descend
abruptly before you have finished work,
it approaches palely waiting for you
to get outside to witness another illumined hour

you feel someone brush against you,
on the street, you smell leather, the lake,
the coming leaves, the rain's immortality
pierces you, but you will be asleep when it arrives

you will lie in the groove of a lover's neck
unconscious, translucent, tendons singing,
and that should be enough, the circumference
of the world narrowed to your simple dreams

Days are perfect, that's the thing about them,
standing here in half darkness, I think this.
It's difficult to rise to that, but I expect it
I expect each molecule of my substance to imitate that

I can't of course, I can't touch syllables
tenderness, throats.
Look it's like this, I'm just like the rest,
limping across the city, flying when I can

what she might collect now and what she isn't
the bristle of light so public and irretrievable
the wood crumbled into paper too appropriate
the grey patch of stars that made her still mouth
the oblivious dress she wore, the shoes
grafted to her feet and the ink-dry pavement
her mourning, lustrous as fury

yet she too had glimpsed herself,
an unrepentant cheekbone, those fingers
brushing glyphs of newsprint away
the extraordinary emptiness of the woman
emerging from clusters of dots on the front page
then the second page, then the last page
then vanishing all together, but not vanished

there, in the time, transparent,
held and held, she had been held, why
it was so quiet there and cool as edges
anything nearing life or what she might do
now, any opening, now again in the bolt
of a bicycle, again she had sensed, glimpsed
herself, now as pitiable and that she could not take

lust she had lost along with the things
in her suitcases that morning, and the things,
the slivers of seconds in between,
fallen, all of it, tinted, sunken, all of it,
that, she wanted back, that at least if not
a daughter as silver as velocity; and the true
taste of things and the atmosphere of her blood

beating at her temples in apprehension or fear
or love or any feeling; the climate of substances
she would have touched, the divine elements
her eyes ought to have seen, her throat devour,
the space surrounding her, look that gesture
of a boy the other morning, even the panic of a woman
bowing out of orbit to a lodestar of crack

once she wore powder blue skirts and embroidered
Indian blouses, then she stood on the corner of
Oakwood and St. Clair waiting for a bus, the clarity
of the traffic, the sky, the day, her life
her directions, plain, unknown, except for this,
the idea, the idea that she was possible
nothing but the sun in the blood of a summer

she used to buy a new pair of sandals
each year, soften the leather with the sweat
of her feet, then a wide-mouthed woven bag
out of which wine and letters and lipstick
and panties, water, apples, bracelets, and grapes
could fall; she went to concerts tasting music
and the cocks of jazz musicians, taking their mouths

in her own scent; she used to jump fire hydrants
on Bloor when darkness wet the roads and drunks
cradled light posts; she used to take ganga-high rides
to Montreal when her body was dangerous and full
of liquid; she could assassinate streets with her eyes
damage books and chemical compounds and honey and waiting
rooms, dance floors would bleed from the knife of her dress

until, it must be said, the moment when all women realize
the war they're in, that the only possibility is falling
that the fragments of winter and music are only solemn
kisses to their half-life and only mercy and surrender move
their hand. Well what's more with a daughter given up
to lightening and pity she wanted her blue skirt back,
she wanted that single sense she'd lost, anticipation

She needed to smell, without dying, the skin
of someone else, she needed without a wounding,
without a murder, without a killing, a truce if not peace,
a city, as a city was supposed to be, forgetful,
and to gather up any charm she might have
left, to sleep, to feel snow, to have it matter,
to wake like leaves, to hate rain

XXXII

Every smell is now a possibility, a young man
passes wreathed in cologne, that is hope;
teenagers, traceries of marijuana, that is hope too, utopia;

smog braids the city where sweet grass used to,
yesterday morning's exhaust, this day's
breathing by the lightness, the heaviness of the soul.

Every night the waste of the city is put out and taken away
to suburban landfills and recycling plants,
and that is the rhythm everyone would prefer in their life,

that the waste is taken out, that what may be useful
be saved and the rest, most of it, the ill of it,
buried.

Sometimes the city's stink is fragrant offal,
sometimes it is putrid. All depends on what wakes you up,
the angular distance of death or the elliptic of living.

XXXIII

From time to time . . . frequently, always
there is the arcing wail of a siren, as seas
hidden in the ordinariness of the city
the stream and crash of things lived
if it is late at night and quiet, as quiet
as a city can get, as still as its murmurous genealogy
you can hear someone's life falling apart

Most people can sleep through a siren. I can't.
It isn't the proximity of it that wakes me, as shores,
it is its emotion. Its prophecy. Even at a great distance
you sense its mortal discoveries
whoever it is calling for, whoever is caught
human, you can hear their gnawed substance in its song

In a siren, the individual muscles of a life collapsing,
as waves, stuttering on some harm,
your fingers may flutter in the viscera of an utter stranger
I wake up to it, open as doorways,
breathless as a coming hour, and undone

ACKNOWLEDGEMENTS

My deepest thanks to Ted Chamberlin for reading this work, and to Leslie Saunders, Rinaldo Walcott, Kwame Dawes, and Leleti Tamu. Also to the Women's Studies Department, Simon Fraser University, without whose support this book would not be possible.